Published by Creative Paperbacks
P.O. Box 227, Mankato, Minnesota 56002
Creative Paperbacks is an imprint of
The Creative Company
www.thecreativecompany.us

Design and production by The Design Lab
Art direction by Rita Marshall
Printed by Corporate Graphics in the
United States of America

Photographs by Dreamstime (Pwozza, Skynesher,
Stephenmeese), Getty Images (Georgette Douwma,
Mustafa Ozer/AFP, Flip Nicklin, Gail Shumway,
Stuart Westmorland, Norbert Wu), and iStockphoto
(Lars Christensen, Jose Manuel Gelpi Diaz, Nancy
Nehring, Tammy Peluso, James Steidl)

The Library of Congress has cataloged the
hardcover edition as follows:
Riggs, Kate.
Dolphins / by Kate Riggs.
p. cm. — (Amazing animals)
Includes index.
Summary: A basic exploration of the appearance,
behavior, and habitat of dolphins, a family of fish-eat-
ing porpoises. Also included is a story from folklore
explaining why dolphins are so friendly.
ISBN 978-1-58341-989-2 (hardcover)
ISBN 978-0-89812-562-7 (pbk)
1. Dolphins—Juvenile literature. I. Title. II. Series.
QL737.C432R55 2011
599.53—dc22   2009047732

CPSIA: 061311 PO1475

9 8 7 6 5 4 3

DOLPHINS

BY KATE RIGGS

CREATIVE
PAPER BACKS

Bottlenose dolphins have mouths that seem to smile

Dolphins are animals that live in the **oceans**. They are some of the smartest animals in the world. There are more than 30 kinds of ocean dolphins. Bottlenose and spinner dolphins are two kinds of dolphins. Common and humpbacked dolphins are other kinds.

oceans big areas of deep, salty water

Dolphins have smooth skin and blowholes, just like whales

Most dolphins have smooth, gray skin. Large fins help them swim through the water. Their noses are shaped like beaks. Dolphins have many small teeth. They breathe through **blowholes** on top of their heads.

blowholes holes in the skin on top of dolphins' heads that open to take in air

The smallest dolphins weigh less than 100 pounds (45 kg). Dolphins like the bottlenose dolphin are bigger. Male bottlenose dolphins weigh more than 1,000 pounds (454 kg)! Females weigh about 600 pounds (272 kg).

Male dolphins are almost always bigger than females

People often see dolphins swimming close to shore

Most dolphins live in salty water. Some live in rivers, too. Dolphins like to swim in warm water. So most live in waters near the equator (*ee-KWAY-ter*), where it is always warm.

equator the middle part of Earth where the weather is the warmest

Dolphins eat food from the ocean. Some of their favorite foods to eat are small fish like mackerels. Sometimes dolphins eat squid and crabs, too.

Dolphins swallow most food without even chewing

Dolphin calves swim close to their mothers to stay safe

A mother dolphin has one **calf** at a time. The calf stays close to its mother. When the calf is about two years old, it starts learning how to hunt. Calves stay with their mothers until they are about six years old. Most wild dolphins can live about 25 years.

calf a baby dolphin

Dolphins live in groups called pods. Small pods have 2 to 15 dolphins. Big pods can have hundreds of dolphins. Dolphins spend a lot of their time swimming and playing.

Dolphins are happiest while near many other dolphins

*A big dolphin pod can
catch and eat many fish*

Dolphins work together to hunt for food. They talk to each other using clicking and whistling sounds. If one dolphin spots a group of fish to eat, it tells the other dolphins.

Today, some people go on boats to see dolphins in the wild. Other people visit zoos to see dolphins. It is exciting to see these smart animals jump out of the water!

Dolphins like to jump high in the air when they play

A Dolphin Story

Why are dolphins friendly to humans? People in Greece used to tell a story about this. Once, a famous singer named Arion was sailing on a boat. There were bad men on the boat who wanted to hurt Arion and take his money. So he jumped overboard. A dolphin saw him and carried him on its back. Arion got to land safely. From then on, dolphins were the friends of humans!

Read More

Pfeffer, Wendy. *Dolphin Talk: Whistles, Clicks, and Clapping Jaws.* New York: HarperCollins, 2003.

Simon, Seymour. *Dolphins.* New York: HarperCollins, 2009.

Web Sites

Dolphins World: Dolphins for Kids
http://www.dolphins-world.com/Dolphins_for_Kids.html
This site has art activities, as well as puzzles about dolphins.

Enchanted Learning: Bottlenose Dolphins
http://www.enchantedlearning.com/subjects/whales/activities/ whaletemplates/bottledolphintemplate.shtml
This site has bottlenose dolphin facts and a picture to color.

Index